Welcome to the Bubble Construction Kit instruction manual.

This was supposed to be a few pages talking abo[ut] tools that you purchased called the Bubble Cons[truction Kit,] a STEM heavy book on the structures of bubble[s.] It was soon realized that this information would be useful for anyone using bubbles regardless if they had just purchased a set of tools or not.

The 'tools' in question were a support frame and three attachments for making bubbles, plus additional equipment. The support frame holds each attachment in the air using a magnet so that a person learning bubble tricks would not have to worry about holding it steady while learning a new trick.

The kit is a fancy frame with a magnet at the top and special steel 'blanks' on each attachment to easily stick onto the magnet. But this could be duplicated with a bit of ingenuity and a way of attaching onto the same bubble tools. A person interested in constructing things with bubbles would certainly be able to construct the frame talked about in this book.

The decision was made to write the book so that it could be sold without the fancy frame and magnets and attachments. People could look at the first few pages of the book and, after a trip to a local hardware store and the bubble section of their favorite toy shop, duplicate everything needed to begin constructing amazing bubble structures.

If you purchased the kit: Assemble the pieces of the frame, set it up, and you now have everything you need to get started on your journey into the amazing world of soap bubbles.

If you purchased this book without the kit: You have a little bit of preparation to do before you get started.

There is a third option. Many people learn these tricks while holding the various attachments in one hand and make the bubble with the other. It takes more practice at first, but eventually you can achieve the same success.

Enjoy your journey! *Thomas C. Altman*

The kit.
These are prototypes, your kit may look different.

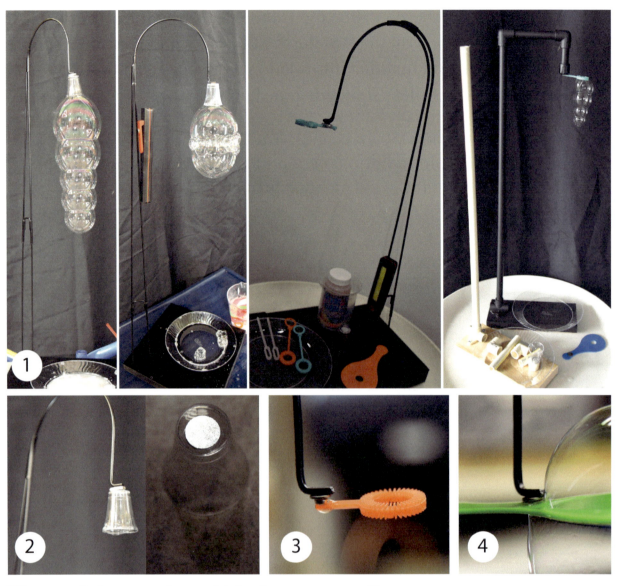

Figure 1.1 *Parts for Bubble Construction Kit*
1. Variations of the support frame with magnet at the top.
2. Hanging cup with steel blank glued to top.
3. Hanging wand with steel blank glued to end.
4. Hanging paddle with steel blank glued on handle.

Figure 1.2 *Additional tools: extra wands, bubble plate, straws, flashlight, professional bubble juice, cup, Ghost bubble pipe*

Build your own

Many bubblers build their own equipment. This is one idea of a kit made with common PVC materials from a hardware store and bubble tools from a toy store.

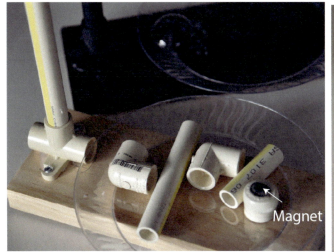

Figure 1.3 *Parts needed to build PVC Bubble Construction Kit*

Build a kit with 1/2 inch PVC pipe and fittings.

- A 'T' fitting or angle fitting that screws into a wooden base will hold a 24 inch (61cm) section of pipe.
- At the top of that pipe place a 90 degree elbow fitting that will hold a 5 inch section of pipe.
- At the end of that piece another 90 degree elbow fitting will hold a 2 inch down section.
- Place a cap fitting with a magnet glued to it at the end of the down section.
- A small plastic cup, half of a bubble wand, and a paddle ball paddle with a hole drilled in it all need to have a steel washer glued to them.
- The pieces of PVC do not need to be glued.
- The 5 inch section, the 90 degree elbow fitting, and the 2 inch down section can be removed and used for the Ghost bubble pipe.
- Purchase the additional wands, some straws of different diameters, a plastic desert plate, a small flashlight, some bubble juice, and a small cup.

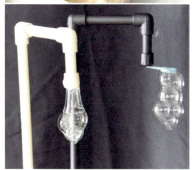

Figure 1.4 *Assembled kit*

Bubble Construction Kit

Building has been an important part of our history. Taking simple materials and arranging them into new and useful shapes is how both humans and nature construct everything from cells to buildings.

In the world of construction a few names stand out, and among them is Buckminster Fuller. He saw buildings shaped like cubes and wondered if they could be shaped like spheres. He made popular the geodesic dome that is seen on playgrounds and future habitats for life on Mars (Figure 1.5).

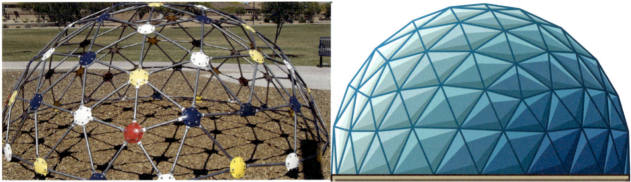

Figure 1.5 *Playground geodesic dome and basic structure for homes*

In the world of bubbles there are a few names that stand out, and among them is Tom Noddy. Noddy saw bubbles that were shaped like spheres and wondered if they could be shaped like cubes, dodecahedra or stars, caterpillars, tornadoes, volcanoes or double carousels spinning in opposite directions. He went on to create a library of bubble structures that have been copied and presented by bubble artists around the world. So quickly did his structures spread that often when performing in new countries people would ask if he had gotten the idea from some local performer who was doing the same structure.

Much of the art form is built on the foundation laid by this man (Figure 1.6).

Figure 1.6 *Tom Noddy and his bubble star structure*
Photo: (Michelle Bates)

- This kit will include tools and step by step instructions to build the most popular of these structures.
- Some of the science and math that make these structures possible will also be discussed.
- Professional bubble artists will demonstrate these structures.

How the Bubble Construction Kit fits education curriculum:

Bubbles encompass the 5E model for guided inquiry

Engage: stimulate interest.
People the world over from young to old have an interest in bubbles. While adults may dismiss bubbles as a child's toy there remains a large population that continue to be fascinated with the physics, math, and science of bubbles. Plus, they are very pretty.

Explore: hands on investigations.
People have been making bubbles for many hundreds of years some quite literally with their hands. This is a project that requires 'hands on' and intuitively leads to further investigation. True experiments are seldom done in schools because of the potential for harm. Soap bubbles are an exception because, even in an extreme event, the participants just get soapy.

Explain: scientific explanations.
Each trick will be explained with different levels of scientific detail. While explanations will try to stay within 'pulling forces' and 'pushing forces' much of the key vocabulary will be highlighted to allow further guided investigation.

Elaborate: new applications.
Bubble tricks build on previous knowledge and each trick described has several popular variations that are used. Examples of how the same basic trick is used and performed by world famous bubble artists is readily available on a variety of social media platforms.

Evaluate: new understanding and skills.
There are few activities that have more universal opportunities for success than blowing bubbles. These activities can teach both quick success and perseverance. 'Failure' is common amongst even the professionals. As world renown bubble artist Tom Noddy often says, "Every bubble I've ever blown has popped."

How to use the Bubble Construction Kit trainer.

Each construction will involve three parts.

> **1.** The first section will be step by step instructions on HOW to do the construction. This will be outlined with a box. Some hints will be included that will help you be successful. Practice each construction until you can do it consistently.

2. The second section will explain some of the science and math of WHY the construction does what it does. This may get a little too complicated from some readers. Don't worry about that.

3. The third section may introduce a professional bubble artist illustrating each construction, or give you insight about how this structure is used within the bubble community.

Some general information about bubbles:

- The bubble tools in this kit must be wet in order to form or support a soap bubble. If you are blowing a bubble and it keeps popping it is likely that it is touching something that is not wet.
- Bubble solutions are made of soap, water, and often an additive to make the mix perform better. Over time the water in a bubble will evaporate, and the bubble will pop on its own. The air temperature and humidity will effect the time it takes for the water to evaporate.
- The colors of a bubble are produced by the thickness of the bubble film. As the water is pulled by gravity, or evaporates, the bubble film will get thinner and the color will change.
- The thin films require a somewhat gentle touch much of the time but being too slow or too gentle will limit what you can do to manipulate them during their short lifespan.
- A quick motion with a wet straw can help you to escape the cling of the bubble when that's a problem.
- You want to use the bubble's affinity for wetness to help you build and manipulate these structures.
- Practice.

Table of Contents:

Bubble Construction Kit	5	Gravity:	32
The Bubble Wand:	9	Using the bubble plate:	33
What makes a bubble form?	10	The bubble dome:	34
Surface tension:	11	Make a side by side bubble:	35
Air pressure:	12	Popping the wall:	36
Soap:	13	Bubble geometry:	37
Polymers:	14	Forces at bubble junctions:	38
Bubble Juice:	15	Dome in a dome:	39
Review; What makes a bubble?	16	Object in a dome:	40
The Bubble Straw:	17	Slow pop bubble:	41
Make a single bubble:	18	Air pressure difference:	42
Forces on the single bubble:	19	Bubble catch:	43
Make a double bubble:	20	Bubbles in a bubble:	44
Make a bubble 'caterpillar':	21	Newton's laws of motion:	45
Make a bubble cube:	22	More bubbles in a bubble:	46
Geometry of the bubble cube:	23	Floating bubble pipe:	47
Tom Noddy's bubble cube:	24	The Ghost Bubble:	48
Examples of the bubble cube:	25	Reflections in bubbles:	49
Make a carousel:	27	Bubble colors:	50
Modified carousel:	28	Photographing bubbles:	51
Stabilize the structure:	29	Make a light table:	52
Bubble puzzle solved:	30	What is next?:	53
The hanging wand:	31	Attributes:	62

Vocabulary terms

Adhesion	Focal point	Newton thin film interference
Air friction	Gravity	Polymer
Air pressure	Guar gum	Soap Bubble Wiki
Bernoulli principle	Inertia	Surface tension
Capillary action	Magnus Effect	Thin Film
Cohesion	Marangoni Effect	Vapor
Equilibrium	Minimum surfaces	

The Bubble Wand:

a) Dip the bubble wand into some bubble juice.

b) Notice the film of soapy water that forms over the wand.

c) Also notice the bubble juice that collects on the wand. This juice will allow you to make more and bigger bubbles.

d) Notice how some of the juice drips off the wand (Figure 1.7). Gravity will continue to pull on the juice even after the bubble has formed.

e) Blow air into the film and watch it make a bubble.

Figure 1.7 *Fresh dipped bubble wand*

- Congratulations. You have participated in an activity that goes back in recorded history at least 400 years, and probably much further. This simple bubble represents a lot of science and fun for children and adults alike.

- We will examine some of the fun things that can be built with bubbles as well as investigate some of the science behind it all.

- You can simply skip all the science and jump right to the different activities. Come back and learn the science later.

Figure 1.8 *Bubbles can be a child's toy, but they are everywhere from the foam bed we sleep on to the model of the universe. Bubble science is even used to study the structure of black holes.*

What makes a bubble form?

Soap bubbles are made from three different components which each contribute to the life of the bubble. These components each contribute 'Forces' to the structure. The final bubble is the result of these forces all being balanced. The balance of forces is known as '**Equilibrium**'.

Water:

The forces that hold water together are called molecular forces. Each water molecule is attracted to other water molecules by these pulling forces. These pulling forces can be thought of as invisible springs holding the water molecules together (Figure 1.9). The actual force is electric in nature.

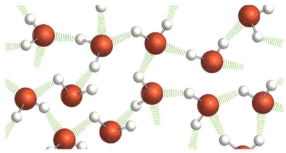

Figure 1.9 *Attractive 'pulling' forces between molecules of water can be thought of as tiny springs.*

If the molecules are moving slowly the structure that forms by these forces can be a crystal (think snowflakes) and it is known as a solid.

Figure 1.10 *Slower moving molecules can form crystals, and faster moving molecules can form spheres.*

As you add energy to the solid (heating) the molecules move faster and if they move fast enough the crystal structures will break (melting). Once enough heat energy is added to the solid it will melt into a liquid. Liquids also have molecular forces, and the structure that forms by these forces can be a sphere (rain drops).

> **a)** Place a drop of water on a dry surface and look closely at the drop that forms. It will have rounded edges at the surface as the molecular forces try to pull all the water together.

Surface tension:

The molecular forces in water, called **cohesion**, act to hold it together. It is these forces in water that pulls it into the curved shape you see for a drop of water on a table, and if it no other forces are acting then it will pull it into a perfect sphere (Figure 1.11).

Figure 1.11 *Water ball in free fall on the international space station in the process of forming a perfect sphere.*

The surface of liquids has an additional force acting on it. Because the water molecules at the surface do not have water molecules above them, the water molecules at the surface tend to attract more strongly with neighboring water molecules (Figure 1.12). This additional pulling force makes the surface of water act differently than the rest of the water in a container, and giving it special properties

Pulling forces are called 'tension' forces, and because it is caused by the surface of a liquid, it is called **surface tension**. Water has the highest surface tension of any liquid besides mercury.

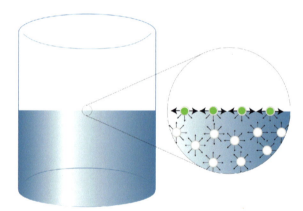

Figure 1.12 *Water molecules at the surface have a stronger cohesion force with neighboring molecules*

- Surface tension has been compared to the stretched surface of a balloon, with the elastic pull of the balloon working against the pressure of the trapped air.
- This comparison can be made with a soap bubble that has the surface tension of the water in the bubble working against the air pressure within the bubble.

But what is air pressure?

Air pressure:

If enough energy is added to the liquid the cohesion force will not be strong enough to hold any structure and it will change into a gas. This can be done quickly (boiling) or slowly (evaporation). The molecules of gases are moving quickly and try to escape into any available space. For some materials this happens at very low temperature so that it is normally a gas. Air is an example of nitrogen and oxygen that are a gas at room temperature. Water vapor (gas) is also part of air.

The pushing of gas molecules creates a force on every part of the container. The gas in a container will push back against any force that tries to squeeze it together. This pushing on a surface is known as pressure, and because it is caused by air, it is known as **air pressure**.

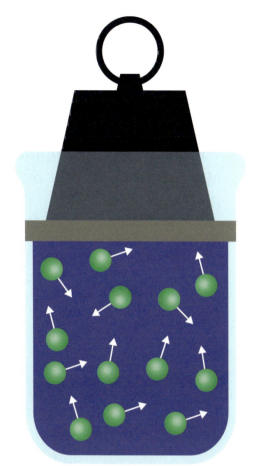

Figure 1.13 *Air pressure pushing back on a weight trying to squeeze it.*

Some places in the world refer to these bubbles as water bubbles because it is the surface tension in the water which balances the air pressure trapped inside to produce the structure you are familiar with.

You may ask yourself, "Why do we add soap to the water?".

The role of soap is important to the formation of larger bubbles and it requires even more science to understand.

Figure 1.14 *A bubble is the result of the air pressure inside equaling the surface tension of the water.*

Soap:

Soap and detergent have interesting molecules. One end of the molecule is attracted to water (hydrophilic), and the rest of the molecule repels water (hydrophobic) (Figure 1.15). When mixed with water the hydrophilic ends will be attracted to the water molecules. This has the effect of spreading the water molecules out a bit and reduce the surface tension of the water.

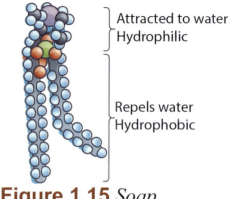

Figure 1.15 *Soap molecule*

a) Place two drops of water on a dry flat surface side by side. Notice the round shape.

b) Put a bit of soap on a tooth pick. Touch the soap to one water drop and observe what happens. Compare the two.

Soapy water can be made to form a thin film. It is this film of water with soap on the top and bottom that will eventually create a bubble (Figure 1.16). This is known as a '**Thin Film**' and there are many science applications to the study of thin films.

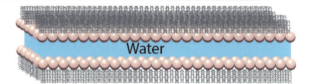

Figure 1.16 *Film of water between two sheets of soap molecules.*

The thin film now has two surfaces of water, top and bottom, so the surface tension is greater in a thin film.

To form a thin film you need some framework that has water on it, and an opening for the film to form. Bubble performers use straws, tubes, frames, or string to form this thin film. You used a bubble wand to produce the same kind of thin film. It is the starting point of all bubbles.

Air pressure is then used to stretch the film into a bubble.
How far it stretches depends upon a number of factors, but the really big bubbles all have a third ingredient, polymers.

Figure 1.17 *Damian Jay, Fareham, UK*

Polymers:

A 'Monomer' is the word for a molecular shape, and a '**Polymer**' means a lot of those shapes connected into a chain (Figure 1.18). There are many types of polymers that can be added to soap and water. They are included to make the bubbles more elastic to make larger and longer lasting bubbles. Scientists studying the effect suggest that the polymers get 'entangled' with the water in the film.

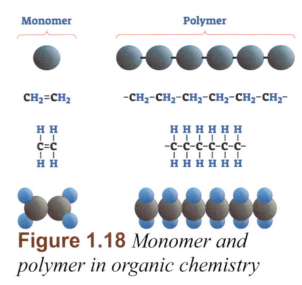

Figure 1.18 *Monomer and polymer in organic chemistry*

a) Mix up some water with a little bit of soap.

b) Use the bubble wand and see how big a bubble you can blow.

c) Try changing the ratio of soap and water. For example, a little more soap with the same amount of water.

d) See if that makes better bubbles or not.

e) Try to find the best ratio of soap to water.

f) Wash off the bubble wand and then use some commercial bubble juice. This will have a special polymer added.

g) Compare the size and number of bubbles that can be made with each mixture.

Polymers make up much of plastic and many manufactured products but natural polymers, like **Guar gum**, are also used in home made bubble mixes.

There is a Soap Bubble Wiki site with many of the popular recipes used by the professionals as well as advice on how to mix each one. Making your own bubble mix is lots of fun.

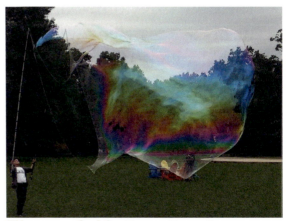

Figure 1.19 *Gary Pearlman in Cleavland Ohio, USA using a Guar based bubble juice.*

Bubble Juice:

Bubble performers often mix up different solutions depending upon what structures they want to make. Many of them simply rely on commercial bubble juice that they can buy at the store. Not all commercial bubble juices perform equally, but for this kit any of them should work.

> a) Commercial bubble juices have been carefully mixed for best results and are not designed to be mixed with other types.
>
> b) Mixing different kinds is an experiment that could be fun.

Figure 1.20 *Melissa Bornmann, Boston USA, using a guar based polymer.*

Figure 1.21 *Bubble made by Rick Findley; Manzanillo Mexico, using his own unique mix.*

As you begin to explore larger and more complex structures you may find that you will have to investigate the mixture to become successful. There are many different sources that can help you. Performers are always searching for the perfect mix and a true professional (Bubbleologist) (Figure 1.21) may just become a practical chemist along the way.

A bubbleologist will consider the relative humidity, air temperature and the dust in the air where they will perform and modify their mix to fit the atmospheric conditions.

But the one thing you find is that the weekend bubble fan or the world famous professional bubble artists are often eager to help new people in their journey through the bubble world. Much of their collective knowledge can be found on the Soap Bubble Wiki.

Review; What makes a bubble?

Equilibrium:

- Remember that a bubble is the result of all these forces being balanced. The pulling forces of the water and polymer will work against the pushing force of the air pressure.
- To form a bubble these forces must be balanced.

a) You need a loop of some material. You want something that will hold a little bubble juice so that as the bubble forms there is more juice to form a larger bubble.

b) Place the loop in the bubble juice and gently pull it out. You will see the water try to hold onto the loop a bit, but when it is pulled enough to overcome this force a film will form on the loop.

c) Just as soon as you pull the loop out of the juice another force, 'Gravity', will try and pull the juice back down (towards the center of the earth).

d) When you blow on the film the air pressure will push on the film and the water forces will try and keep the film flat.

e) If you blow too hard the force of air pressure will be much greater than the force of the film and it will break.

f) If you blow too gently the force of the film will be able to resist the force of pressure.

g) Find a speed that allows the air pressure to stretch the film without breaking it. This will cause the film to get thinner and stretch outward. If there is enough juice on the wand then this film will get bigger and bigger.

h) Eventually the sides of the film will try and pull it back together and, if you balanced everything, the film will once again come together trapping some air inside.

i) This is a bubble. The air pressure inside will push on the sides of the film trying to push out. The water force of the film will try and pull inward. The resultant bubble is the balance of those forces.

j) The bubble will float to the ground because of the pull of gravity.

The Bubble Straw:

a) Dip one end of a straw in the bubble juice. When it is pulled out a film can form (Figure 1.22).

b) Hold it up and blow through the straw.

c) If you blow quickly, you can get some tiny bubbles.

d) If you blow slowly, you can make a large bubble.

e) If you blow hard enough you can clear the straw of soap and just blow air.

f) You can break this film by sucking in on the straw quickly. This will prove to be a very useful skill.

Figure 1.22 *Bubble straw with soap film on the end.*

Capillary action:

There is another force to consider. When fluids are next to a surface they experience an attractive force, called **adhesion**. This is seen with straws put into water (Figure 1.23). Some water will move up against the pull of gravity. This is known as **capillary action** and it can exert a force to 'hold' bubble juice in a straw.

Capillary action is why liquids can soak into a cloth or anything with small fibers. Your bubble wand has little grooves cut into the ring to hold extra juice using the adhesive force of capillary action (Figure 1.24).

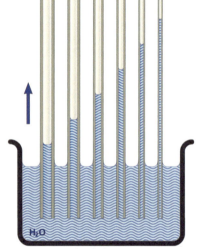

Figure 1.23 *Capillary action with straws*

Bubble artists or hobbyists often make their own bubble wands. They take a plastic or metal ring and wrap it with an absorbent material so that it will hold more bubble juice and produce bigger bubbles.

Figure 1.24 *Capillary action with bubble wand*

Make a single bubble:

a) Put the hanging cup on the holder after first dipping it into your soap solution.

b) Place the end of a straw in the soap solution.

c) Bring the straw to the hanging cup and gently blow a bubble.

d) If the bubble does not stick to the hanging cup, then blow another one so that the edge of the bubble touches the cup.

e) Pull the straw away with a swift move sideways. This should leave the bubble on the cup.

f) Practice.

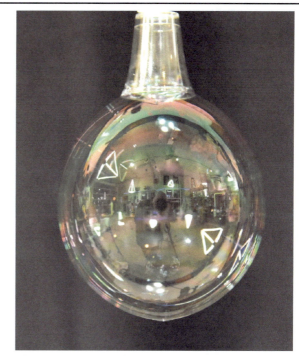

Figure 1.25 *Single bubble*

Things to work on while you practice

- Make the bubble quickly. Some tricks will require you to make a number of bubbles before the first one pops.
- Make bubbles the same size. There are structures that look better if all the bubbles are the same size. Learn to measure your breath and to control how much you breath out.
- Make large bubbles and make small bubbles. Some structures require both.
- Watch the bubble over its entire life. Notice that the colors change, and how the colors change. With a little practice you should be able to predict when the bubble will pop naturally.
- Watch what happens to the bubble when you pull the straw away. Move it quickly and slowly and see what difference that makes. Pull it down or pull it away and see what happens. Learn to control the way your bubble moves using the straw.

Forces on the single bubble:

- Gravity can be thought of as a force that pulls towards the center of the earth.
- The hanging cup allows the bubble to remain in place with an upward force.
- This upward force is produced by the adhesion of the fluid on the cup and cohesion of the water in the bubble with the water on the cup.
- The bubble is not perfectly round because the cup changes the shape, but the air inside the bubble has mass, as well as the fluid in the film, and they are both being pulled downward by gravity. This effect is exaggerated in (Figure 1.26).
- Air pressure pushes outward on the bubble.
- Molecular attraction of water pulls inward on the bubble.
- All these forces are working at the same time and, if in equilibrium, the bubble will remain.

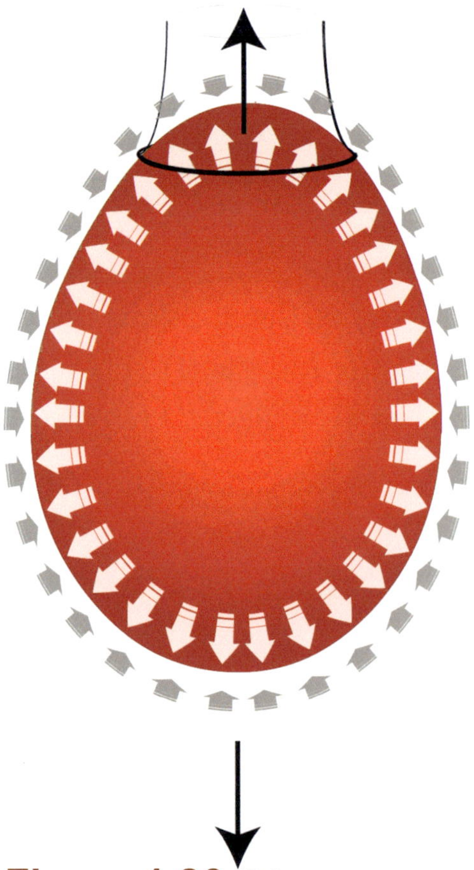

Figure 1.26 *Diagram of forces on the bubble. Upward force from the cup, downward force of gravity, Outward force of air pressure, inward force of surface tension.*

As the bubble hangs there you can observe changes.

1. The water in the bubble will start to move downward. You can see color changes in the bubble as the result of the thin film getting thinner.
2. Water will evaporate into the air also making the bubble thinner.

If a drop of water appears at the bottom of the bubble it will drag the bubble downward. You can touch this drop with the end of your wet straw and remove it.

> **a)** Notice what happens to the bubble when you remove that drop on the bottom.

Make a double bubble:

a) Put the hanging cup on the holder after first dipping it into your soap solution.

b) Place the end of a straw in the soap solution.

c) Bring the straw to the hanging cup and gently blow a bubble.

d) Pull the straw away with a swift move sideways. This will leave the bubble on the cup.

e) Re dip your straw in the soap solution.

f) Bring the straw to the bottom of the first bubble.

g) Gently blow a second bubble so that it attaches to the first bubble.

h) Pull the straw away.

i) Practice.

Figure 1.27 *Double bubble*

- If certain conditions are met then bubbles can share water (and soap). When this happens the energy of the structure is less than the two single bubbles.
- This means that the equilibrium requirements change a little with the pressure from the top bubble and bottom bubble creating a wall between them.
- This wall is a shared surface for both bubbles.
- The addition of a second bubble below the first increases the weight that must be supported by the cup.

As we shall see, bubbles can form complex shapes. In mathematics there is a branch of study called '**minimum surfaces**' that deals with the least material to encompass the largest volume. Bubbles are examples of minimum surface structures.

Make a bubble 'caterpillar':

a) Blow a bubble on the cup.

b) At the bottom of the bubble a drop may form as the water is pulled downward by gravity.

c) You can use this drop to blow another bubble below the first one.

d) Repeat this process to blow a third bubble below the first two.

e) See how many bubbles you can make in a chain. The lower bubbles will pull more on the top one, so make them smaller so they don't weigh as much.

f) Practice.

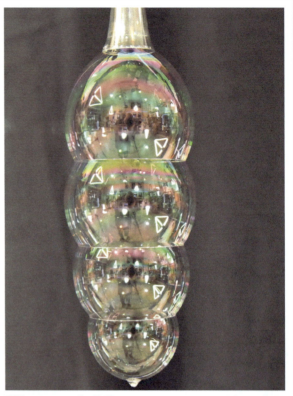

Figure 1.28 *"Caterpillar" bubble*

Professional bubble artists practice this structures using a wand in one hand and a straw in the other. They can move the wand back and forth and make the caterpillar 'dance'.

Figure 1.30 *Sam Heath at a show in London, England.*

Figure 1.29 *Aramis Gehberger in Vienna, Austria*

Make a bubble cube:

a) Blow a bubble on the cup.
b) Blow an equal sized bubble below it.
c) Blow an equal sized bubble at the junction between the top and bottom bubbles.
d) Blow three more equal size bubbles at the same junction.
e) Make sure enough of the straw is wet so that no dry parts touch bubbles.
f) Push it into the center of the six bubbles and carefully blow a bubble in the middle.
g) The middle bubble will form a 'spherical' cube.

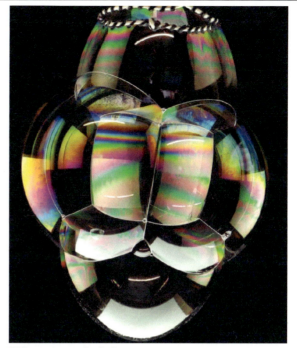

Figure 1.31 *Bubble cube built on larger wand, built and photographed by Martin Cattani Dorelo*

- At this point you will notice that it sometimes the bubbles are difficult to control. You probably saw that with the bubble caterpillar. The liquid on the straw will help you hold the bubble and even allow you to move it around the middle of the structure.

- When you pull the straw away slowly it will stretch the bubble and, when it releases, the bubble will bounce back, sometimes contacting other bubbles or even the frame holding the cup. Practice pulling away the straw quickly.

When bubble entertainers build this structure they use a special device, a mini fog machine, to blow **vapor** into the cube bubble so that it stands out better.

Some even add helium to the top bubble so that it will float (Figure 1.32).

Figure 1.32 *Louis Pearl, USA, using both vapor and helium to make a floating bubble cube*

Geometry of the bubble cube:

- If you examine a cube you will notice that it has six equal faces (Figure 1.33).
- You have also seen that two bubbles connected to each other will produce a single shared wall.
- The bubble cube is made with a bubble in the center that is sharing a wall with six different bubbles.
- The result is a bubble with six sides, or a cube.

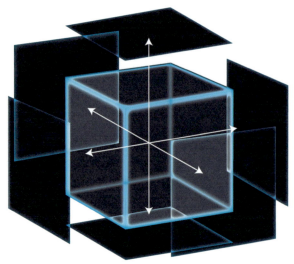

Figure 1.33 *Six faces of a cube*

If you examine one of the walls of a bubble cube you will notice that the edges are not straight (Figure 1.34). The shape is the result of forces trying to find equilibrium. Add another bubble to the structure and observe how thing change.

a) Make a bubble cube.
b) Now add another bubble to the side of the cube.
c) Observe what happens to the inner bubble.

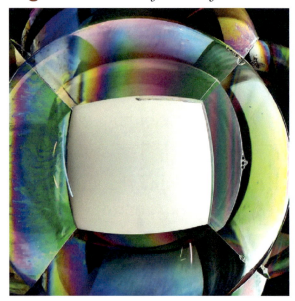

Figure 1.34 *Curved walls of cube (Martin Cattani Dorelo)*

A popular way to make a bubble cube is with a frame with six sides. (This is often done with straws connected with string.) If you place it into some bubble juice and then carefully pull it out, each of the frames will build a film. The surface tension of the films will often draw the six sides together and can trap a cube bubble in the center (Figure 1.35).

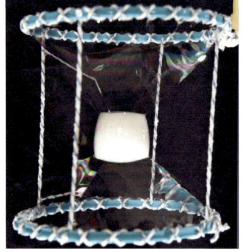

Figure 1.35 *Bubble cube made with a frame*

Tom Noddy's bubble cube:

Tom McAllister, using the stage name of Tom Noddy, changed the face of bubble performance when he went on American and then international television and demonstrated the bubble cube and other structures he had been developing for years.

Figure 1.36 *Tom Noddy displaying a variation of perhaps his most famous structure (Michelle Bates)*

Noddy's gentle humor and simple tools entertained, amazed, and inspired millions across the world. He traveled to science museums, math conferences, colleges, and theaters sharing the 'magic' of bubbles. Fifty years later he continues performing, encouraging both beginners and experts.

He often gives tips to help people perform the tricks, but emphasizes the pursuit of the beauty of the bubble. Other bubble artists still remember his advice:

"Simply make an effort to blow a big bubble and hold it on the wand in front of your eyes and watch it... Watch it until it pops. And then do that again. And then again."

Examples of the bubble cube:

Caroline Cornelius-Jones, Singapore

Eran Backler: Auckland, New Zealand

Dustin Reudelhuber, Tulsa, Oklahoma, USA

Rick Findley, Guadalajara, Mexico

Umar Shoaib, Manchester, England and Pierre-Yves Fusier, Paris France

Helen Dutch; Annan, Dumfriesshire, Scotland

Even more cubes:

Clotilde Cloe, Montreal, Québec, Canada

Chang Yu Te, Taiwan

Meadow Perry, Philadelphia, PA, USA showing the device she uses to put vapor into the cube.

Greg Brinchault; Rennes, France

Matěj Kodeš; Prague, Czech Republic

Make a carousel:

a) Blow a bubble on the cup.

b) Blow an equal sized bubble below it.

c) Blow a smaller bubble at the junction between the top and bottom bubbles.

d) Blow enough small sized bubbles at the same junction so that they complete a ring around the middle of the top and bottom bubbles.

e) Suck on the straw a little to clear the straw, then gently blow on the edge of the ring.

f) The entire structure will rotate as you blow on the edge.

g) Be gentle so as not to blow the structure apart.

h) Practice.

Figure 1.37 *Carousel*

- Breath control becomes very important when making the carousel.
- You notice that the force of your breath can move the bubble as well as create unwanted bubbles.
- Practice making this structure and the cube structure.
- Both of these are part of the routine for almost all bubble performers (Figure 1.38). For doing birthday parties the small wands will do, but when doing large stage shows a large wand and large carousel is always a crowd favorite.

Figure 1.38 *Aramis Gehberger in Vienna, Austria displaying a large carousel made from a hand held wand*

Modified carousel:

By experimenting many 'discover' new structures that are very interesting. If you make something by 'accident', but you like the way it looks, then try and do it again. A popular modification is to add a center to the carousel.

Add a center to the carousel:

a) Make a carousel.

b) Make sure the straw is wet.

c) Push it in between the top and bottom bubbles and blow a bubble that grows until it touches all the bubbles in the ring.

d) This gives the carousel a little more 'character'.

e) Practice.

Figure 1.39 *Carousel with inflated center*

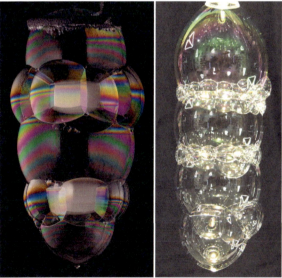

Figure 1.40 *Adding layers to the carousel (Graham Maxwell)*

Figure 1.41 *Caroline Cornelius-Jones using a support frame and modifying a carousel*

The carousel is the ideal structure to begin exploring modifications (Figure 1.40) to create your own structures.

Figure 1.41 shows Caroline Cornelius-Jones using a large support frame to modify an impressive carousel with vapor bubbles and additional structures. She incorporates these with costumes and stories to create a fantasy experience for audiences around the world.

Stabilize the structure:

As you were trying these structures you may have noticed that they moved around every time you blew on the straw, and sometimes the weight of previously made bubbles tear away from the cup.

You can use a bubble wand below the structure to hold the bubbles in place as you add additional bubbles to a structure.

Figure 1.42 *Using bubble wand to support structure*

The wand has some advantages over the cup.

- It has more surface area so that it 'holds' onto the bubble with more force. In fact, many bubble performers use two wands to hold their bubbles, especially when making large structures (Figure 1.43).
- There are more ridges on the wand so that capillary action will hold more bubble juice to allow you to make bigger bubbles.
- The wand can be used to blow the bubble without needing a straw.

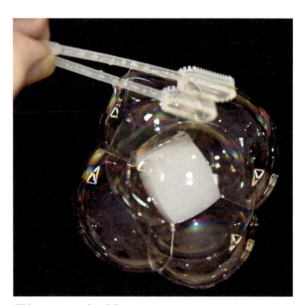

Figure 1.43 *Two wands to hold bubble cube*

The cup has a few advantages over the wand, especially for people just learning the tricks.

- It has a defined ridge that held the bubble in place a bit better.
- It is held in place by the stand so that you do not need to worry about holding the bubble with one hand while learning the trick with the other.

Bubble puzzle solved:

Faris Nasir is a bubbleologist based in Malaysia and has dabbled in the art form since 2010. Inspired by the physics of soap bubbles, he started working with 3D fractal visualizations and found computer software that took a standard 4-6 Duoprism and constructed it with bubble shapes (Figure 1.44).

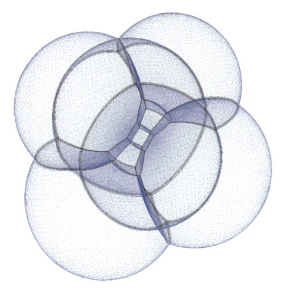

Figure 1.44 *4-6 Duoprism computer model*

Faris attempted to recreate the shape with actual bubbles but found it impossible. The bubble cube was easy, and putting a second cube above the first one was tricky, but he found that the surface tension between the two cubes was too great to allow a third cube to be inserted.

After much effort Faris succeeded (Figure 1.45) by using a second wand on the bottom bubble, and pulling downward on the structure. This stretching force reduced the force between the two cubes and allowed him to insert a third into the total form.

Figure 1.45 *Three cube bubble puzzle solved by Faris Nasir*

The hanging wand:

The hanging wand combines the support of the cup with the practical application of the standard bubble wand.

a) Dip the hanging wand in bubble juice. Attach it to the magnet.

b) Blow a single bubble below the hanging wand.

c) Notice how the fluid flows around the wand.

d) The bubble may have a little more movement on the wand that it did on the cup. It takes some practice to control a bubble on the wand.

e) Blow a second bubble under the first bubble.

f) See how long a caterpillar you can make using the hanging wand.

g) Now try to make a bubble cube using the hanging wand.

h) You may have to make smaller bubbles so that the total weight of the structure does not pull it from the wand.

i) There is a balance between too much fluid on the wand and it being too dry. When you find the perfect balance the surface tension and capillary action of the wand will help hold the bubble structure long enough to complete it.

Figure 1.46 *Hanging wand*

Figure 1.47 *Hanging wand with bubble*

Figure 1.48 *Hanging wand with cube*

Gravity:

a) **Gravity** can be thought of as a force that pulls everything towards the center of the earth.

b) The nature of gravity has been studied for many years, but the effect of gravity is clear to everyone.

c) Gravity works on an object's mass and gives it weight. The bubble fluid has weight and pulls on the bubble. Air also has mass but not nearly as much as the soap solution.

d) The drop that forms at the bottom of your structures (Figure 1.49) can pull it away from the wand before you are done.

Figure 1.49 *Gravity creating water drop that stretches top bubble*

- You have already learned a trick to eliminate this drop; touch it with your straw, and as you practice you will learn to look for this drop before it is too late.

- Performers who do very long caterpillar bubbles will often deliberately pop the one on the bottom to eliminate the additional weight of the accumulated fluid that 'falls' from the string of bubbles.

- As your bubbles get bigger and your structures get more complicated the weight problem increases. There are several solutions to this problem.

a) Use a two wands or a bigger wand at the top. The increased surface area provides a much greater upward force. With a very large wand you can create some very impressive bubbles.

b) Keep your bubbles very small. When bubble performers get together they sometimes have contests to see who can make the smallest cube, or the smallest carousel.

c) Build your bubbles on a wet plate that is already on a table.

Using the bubble plate:

Make sure the entire plate is wet, including the edges. If bubbles pop while using the plate check for dry spots. A small spray bottle may help.

Make a dome:

a) Select a larger diameter straw.

b) Begin to blow a bubble on the edge of the plate and continue until it fills the entire plate with a large bubble dome.

c) Remember that as the bubble grows it may move up along the straw. If it hits a dry spot on the straw the bubble will burst.

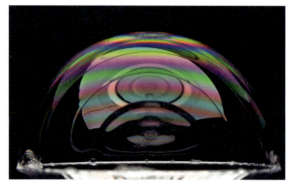

Figure 1.50 *Bubble dome with lighting and showing color bands*

Depending upon the size of the bubble you may have run out of breath. You can use the **Bernoulli principle** to solve this problem.

When a fluid (air or liquid) is moving it creates low pressure on the sides of the flowing fluid. If you are blowing air into a straw, but your mouth is not directly on the straw, a bit of extra air will be drawn

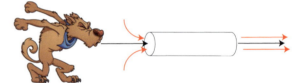

Figure 1.51 *Bernoulli's principle moves extra air*

into the stream. This means that more air can come out of the end of the straw than you are blowing out of your mouth (Figure 1.51).

Demonstration of the Bernoulli principle (Figure 1.52).

a) Take a piece of paper.

b) Blow across the top of the paper and see what happens.

c) The paper is pushed upward by the higher pressure air below it.

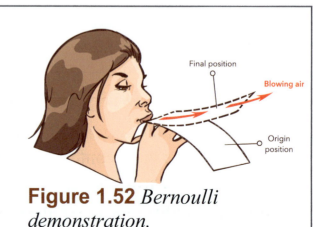

Figure 1.52 *Bernoulli demonstration.*

The bubble dome:

- The bubble plate is another very popular tool for performers. Often they contain lights that illuminate the bubble so that the form is visible and the colors are reflected well (Figure 1.53).
- When the plate contains lights it is called a 'light table'.
- Depending upon the size of the plate the bubbles can be made very large, but the entire plate must be wet for bubbles to form.

Figure 1.53 *Eran Backler using a bubble plate.*

a) Blow the largest bubble you can on your bubble plate.

b) Move your light around the base of the plate and observe the colors reflected.

c) Find a spot that gives you the best view.

d) Closely watch the bubble until it pops on its own.

Things you can see while looking at the bubble.

- **Marangoni Effect**. As gravity pulls water down, and water evaporates from the bubble, the surface tension at some places changes. This imbalance of forces produces movement and is known as the Marangoni Effect. This produces the swirling colors as the thickness of the film changes.

- Eventually the areas at the top will get so thin that light no longer reflects off of it. Issac Newton first identified this region a 'Black film' (Figure 1.54). This can be an indication that the bubble will soon be too thin to support the structure and will pop.

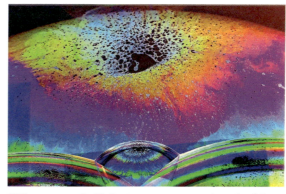

Figure 1.54 *'Newton Black film' at top of dome*

Make a side by side bubble:

a) Blow a bubble onto the plate.

b) Make it large enough to cover more than half of the plate.

c) Remove the straw and then blow a second bubble next to the first one.

d) Try to make the two bubbles the same size so that together they cover the plate.

e) You will see a flat 'wall' between the two bubbles where they share a side and the pressure from one bubble matches the pressure from the other.

f) As you look at this flat side in the light, change your viewing angle until you can see the colors of the bubble.

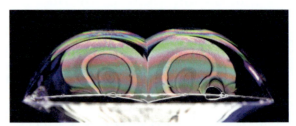

Figure 1.55 *Side by side bubble*

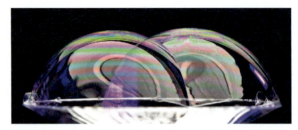

Figure 1.56 *Side by side bubble from a different angle*

- The flat shared wall, when lit properly, can reveal some of the amazing dynamics of forces that are working within the bubble. If you look closely you can observe the Marangoni effect (Figure 1.57) easily.

- Sometimes the two bubbles will not share a wall right away. Keep in mind that the surface of the bubble is covered with soap molecules. There needs to be enough force between the bubbles to push through the soap so that the molecules of water can interact.

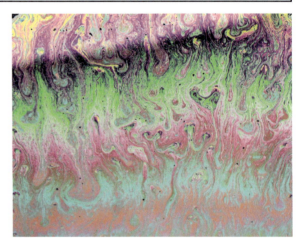

Figure 1.57 *Marangoni effect on the shared wall*

a) Make a smaller bubble next to a larger bubble and observe the shape that is created when they join together.

Popping the wall:

a) The wall separating your two sides of the side by side bubble can be popped while keeping the bubbles intact. This will cause a single large bubble to form.

b) Make sure your straw is wet along as much of its length as needed for this 'trick'.

c) Stick the straw into the bubble until it is touching the shared wall (Figure 1.58).

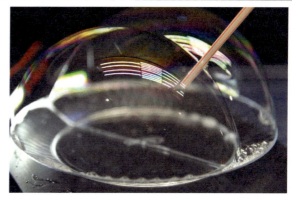

Figure 1.58 *Straw placed in boundary separating bubbles*

d) Quickly suck in on the straw. This quick pressure will break the wall but keep the larger part of the bubble intact.

e) A trick is to put your tongue on the end of the straw, suck in a bit, and then remove your tongue. Try to get a quick force acting on the bubble wall.

f) This action will cause the large bubble to move. If it moves to a dry spot on your straw it will pop that bubble too.

g) This trick can be used to pop a wall between any two bubbles. Try blowing two hanging bubbles from your hanging cup. Put the straw on the wall between the two bubbles and try and pop that wall. Remember, the new bubble will be larger and may grow to hit a dry spot on your straw.

h) Practice.

Popping a wall is one of the special tricks of the bubble performer. This seems almost magical when a person, who does not know this secret, sees

Figure 1.59 *Popping a vapor bubble*

two bubbles turn into one. An extremely popular structure uses a clear bubble with a vapor bubble below it. By breaking the barrier between the two, a vapor cloud forms on the bottom of the new bubble (Figure 1.59). This has many uses for fancy tricks.

Bubble geometry:

a) Blow three equal sized bubbles on the surface of the plate.

b) Look just at the shape that is made by the bottom edge of the bubble where it touches the plate.

c) At the junction where three bubble walls come together they will form an angle of 120 degrees (Figure 1.60) with each other.

d) Now blow four equal sized bubbles on the surface of the plate. What kind of shape do you see?

e) Try to blow a bubble in the center of the four bubbles (Figure 1.61). How would you describe that shape?

f) Keep adding bubbles to the plate and trying to blow bubbles in the middle (Figure 1.62).

g) Record your observations and look for patterns that may help you repeat a structure.

h) See if you can come up with a rule that explains the geometry of bubble junctions.

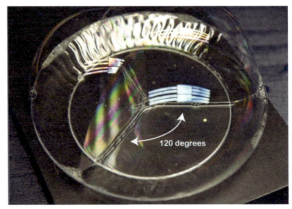

Figure 1.60 *Three bubbles form 120 degrees on the plate*

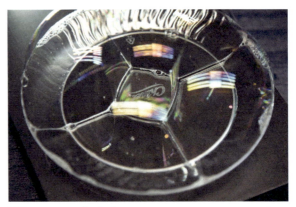

Figure 1.61 *Four bubbles with one bubble in the middle*

Figure 1.62 *Continue to add bubbles to a ring with a central bubble*

- As you continue to add bubbles to the ring and try and put a central bubble in the center (Figure 1.62) bubbles will start to move upwards creating a pile of bubbles. This reveals something else about the forces that are acting between the plate and the other bubbles.

Forces at bubble junctions:

The sphere is the shape formed when the bubble is in equilibrium with no external forces. This shape also has the least amount of surface area that encloses the most amount of volume, known as minimal surface.

The side by side bubble has been a tricky mathematical problem for over a hundred years. In the mathematical theory of minimal surfaces, the double bubble theorem states that the shape that encloses and separates two given volumes and has the minimum possible surface area are three spherical surfaces meeting at angles of 120 degrees.

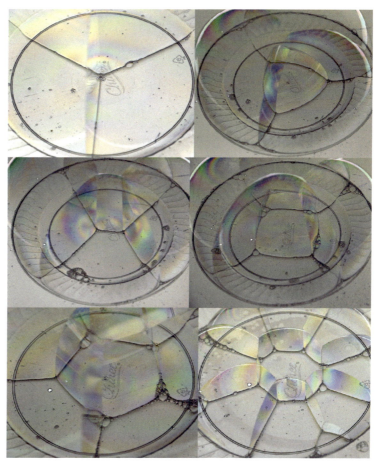

Figure 1.63 *Bubble junctions photographed on a polarizing light table to better illustrate the junctions.*

- This is a fancy way of saying what can be easily observed. When bubbles come together at equilibrium the junction of their walls will be at an angle of 120 degrees (Figure 1.63).

- When squeezed together the pressure forces will cause them to spread out, even pushing the bubble upwards into a pile trying to reach equilibrium.

- Bubbles can be enjoyed without knowing any of the math that explains why they form the shapes you see (Figure 1.64). But the math can be fun too.

Figure 1.64 *Young mathematician studying the double bubble theorem using practical tools.*

Dome in a dome:

a) Blow a bubble dome that fills most of the plate.

b) Make sure your straw is wet along the length that you will put into the dome.

c) Put the end of the straw at the center of the plate and blow another smaller dome.

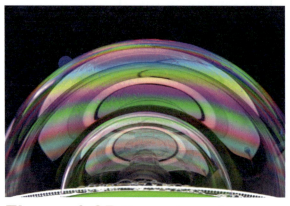

Figure 1.65 *Dome in a dome*

d) Quickly but carefully remove your straw from both domes. This may be the most difficult part of the trick.

e) If the plate is too wet then the inner bubble will move and merge with the outer bubble. If two domes touch the wet straw at the same place they will join together.

f) Start off small at first to get the feel for how the inner dome will move.

g) Remember that each time you blow an inner dome the outer dome will get a bit bigger. If it hits a dry spot on the straw it will pop.

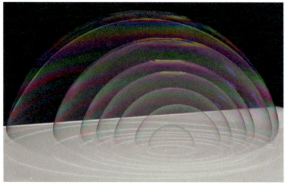

Figure 1.66 *Seven domes*

h) Practice. (The world record is 15 domes inside of domes).

- Variations of the dome in dome trick are also a very popular with bubble entertainers.
- This can be done on any flat surface that is wet. Many people use a sponge to help wet the surface.
- Figure 1.67 shows the dramatic effect of the dome in a dome structure on a light table.

Figure 1.67 *Stephanie Krawinkler, (Milena Novak)*

Object in a dome:

a) Completely wet a plate and a glass or plastic object.

b) Place the object in center of plate.

c) Blow a bubble starting at one edge of a plate and continue until it begins to push over the object in the center (Figure 1.68).

d) You can also start by blowing the bubble near the base of the object and pulling the straw back as the bubble grows.

e) This object will provide a force that pushes back over the bubble. It may take a bit of practice to overcome that force.

f) If any part of the object is not wet the bubble will pop at this point.

g) Continue to blow the bubble until it completely covers the object (Figure 1.69).

Figure 1.68 *Bubble going over a wet object.*

Figure 1.69 *Wet object completely inside bubble*

The soap bubble walls can demonstrate thin film colors, but they also can reflect light like any surface (Figure 1.70). Bubble artists can take advantage of this to create wonderful optical structures.

Figure 1.70 *Three bubbles with image of object reflected in shared wall, (enlarged).*

a) Put a small wet object in the middle of the plate.

b) Create three bubbles that meet in the middle of the plate.

c) Observe the reflected image produced in the shared walls.

Slow pop bubble:

There is a tool that is a cross between a plate and a wand: The paddle. This device must also be wet for a bubble to form on it.

a) Put the bubble paddle on the frame after first making sure it is wet.

b) Blow a small bubble on the top of the paddle (Figure 1.71).

c) If the bubble expands enough to touch the support frame it may pop.

d) Make sure any part of the frame that makes contact with the bubble is also wet.

Figure 1.71 *Hanging paddle with bubble on top*

a) Make sure the bottom of the bubble paddle is wet.

b) Blow a bubble on the bottom of the paddle (Figure 1.72).

c) This may be a larger bubble because gravity will help and there is no frame to interfere with the bubble.

d) Pop the film that covers the hole in the paddle. The air will come out of the bubble slowly.

Figure 1.72 *Hanging plate with bubble on bottom*

- This can be used with any wand. The film that remains across the wand after a large bubble is formed is still part of the bubble. Carefully popping the smaller film across the wand is like putting a small hole in the big bubble.

- This is another popular technique used by bubble artists.

Figure 1.73 *Popping the film*

Air pressure difference:

a) Blow a bubble above and below the paddle.

b) Suck on the straw to pop the film that is shared between the two bubbles at the opening of the paddle (Figure 1.74).

c) Remember to make sure the length of the straw is completely wet.

d) This is similar to popping the wall, but the results will be different.

e) Observe what happens. Is this what you expect?

Figure 1.74 *Popping the film between two bubbles*

- This is a common question in physics classes.
- It is expected that the air in the bigger bubble will fill the smaller bubble until they are both the same size.
- Pressure is a measure of force divided by area. The force of surface tension will be the same for both but the bubble with the smallest AREA will have the higher pressure.
- The higher pressure air in the small bubble will flow into the lower pressure air in the large bubble.

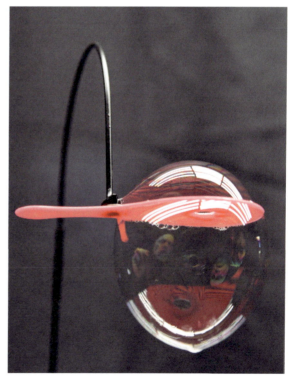

Figure 1.75 *Smaller bubble empties into the larger bubble*

a) Blow two bubbles that are as close to the same size as possible, then pop the film. See what happens.

Bubble catch:

Being able to control a bubble when it is on a wand takes some practice. Being able to control a bubble while it is floating free in the air takes even more practice.

a) Get a paddle wet but do not put it onto the support stand.

b) Use a straw or wand to blow a bubble onto the paddle.

c) Gently blow on the paddle at the point where the edge touches the paddle (Figure 1.76).

d) If you blow hard enough the bubble will fly off the end of the paddle.

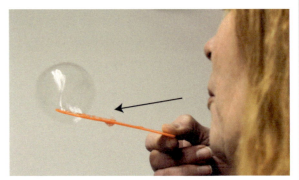

Figure 1.76 *Blowing a bubble off of the paddle*

- This may take a bit of practice.
- The bubble will slowly fall to the floor. Gravity pulls downward on the bubble and the air in the room keeps it from falling too quickly.
- If you are fast enough you can 'catch' the bubble back on the paddle.
- If you caught the bubble you can now 'launch' it back into the air.

a) See how many times you can catch and launch the same bubble.

Why does the bubble fall slowly?

- Although you cannot see it, the room is filled with air. This air is made up of molecules that have mass. A characteristic of mass is that it requires a force to move it. This is called **inertia**.
- For anything to fall it must push the air out of the way on its way to the floor. The force required to overcome this inertia is called **air friction**.
- A coin has weight and it does not have to push a lot of air out of its path, so it falls quickly.
- When you drop a bubble it does not have much mass, so it does not have much weight to push the air out of the way, and it has to push more air out of the way than a coin, so it takes more time to reach the floor.

Bubbles in a bubble:

This structure requires a wand and two different diameter straws.

a) Dip a wand and a larger diameter straw into the bubble juice.

b) Hold the wand in one hand and use the straw to blow a large bubble below the wand.

c) As you do this you will notice that the bubble you are blowing will move in response to the air you are putting into the bubble (Figure 1.77).

Figure 1.77 *Air stream from the straw changing the shape of the bubble.*

d) When the bubble is large enough quickly pull the straw away, leaving the bubble to settle into its spherical shape.

e) Pick up a smaller diameter straw.

f) Bring the straw near the bubble but try not to touch the bubble wall with the straw.

g) Blow a quick burst of air with the straw. This can be done by putting your tongue on the end of the straw, building up a bit of pressure, and then release a short burst. This movement is similar to saying the word 'tut'.

Figure 1.78 *Small bubbles floating inside a larger bubble*

h) One or more small bubbles can form inside of the larger bubble (Figure 1.78). They will eventually float to the bottom and likely merge with the large bubble.

i) The large bubble will want to move too. The structure is easier to build if you use a larger bubble because it will not move as much.

j) Practice.

Newton's laws of motion:

- The air in the bubble has inertia and it does not want to move.
- Newton's second law defines the force needed to overcome that inertia.
- Force is a push (or pull) needed to speed something up, slow it down, or change its direction. This is known as a change in velocity.
- The variables of force can be shown in a simple equation (1.1). The force is equal to the mass (m) being moved, multiplied by how much its velocity is changing (Δv), and both of them divided by the time it takes to change the velocity.
- This says that you can get more force with a quick burst of air than with a slow burst of air.

Figure 1.79 *Force of air pushing into wall of bubble*

$$F = \frac{m \cdot \Delta V}{t}$$

1.1 *Force*

If a slower burst of air strikes the bubble it may produce smaller bubbles, but it may not be enough to overcome the inertia of the entire bubble, but deform it (Figure 1.79) and cause it to burst or to fly off of the wand.

Figure 1.80 *A quick burst of air pushes into the bubble film*

When a quick burst of air is used, and that force is applied to a small spot on the surface of the bubble it can push it inwards while the rest of the bubble stays still. This is how you can blow a small bubble into a larger bubble. With practice you can do this without using a straw.

More bubbles in a bubble:

- The bubbles in a bubble structure can be built with any large bubble.
- Stephanie (Figure 1.81) is using a tri-string wand to make a large bubble, and then blow bubbles into it. Shirley (Figure 1.82) is blowing bubbles into a floating bubble likely formed by a tri-string.
- Corinne (Figure 1.83) used a large wand to create and hold the large bubble.
- They each use quick bursts of air focused on a small spot on the bubble wall to create the smaller 'internal' bubbles.

Figure 1.81 *Stephanie Krawinkler*

Figure 1.82 *Shirley Freeman*

Figure 1.83 *Corinne Bubblespowder, Berlin, Germany*

Floating bubble pipe:

a) Dip the shorter end of the bubble pipe into some bubble juice.

b) Hold it so the end is straight up in the air and gently blow a softball sized bubble.

c) Twist the end of the pipe sideways (Figure 1.84) to release the bubble into the air.

d) Quickly suck air into the pipe to clear any film off the end.

e) Gently blow on the bottom of the bubble and try and keep it in the air (Figure 1.85).

f) With practice you can float the bubble in front of you until it pops naturally.

Figure 1.84 *Twist pipe to release bubble*

- When controlling the bubble you may notice that by blowing on the right side of the bubble you can get the bubble to move to the right.

- The air flow on the right creates a low pressure, and the higher air pressure on the left will push on the bubble. This is shown as BF in Figure 1.86 and it is the result of the Bernoulli effect.

- However, you will also cause the bubble to spin, and that introduces another force that can be used to control the bubble, also moving it to the right.

- This movement is because of the **Magnus Effect** and it produces a force, labeled MF in Figure 1.86. This is the reaction to some air being spun over the top of the bubble, and to the left.

- The Magnus Effect is responsible for causing spinning balls to move off of their normal path. It is used in ping pong, soccer, and golf.

Figure 1.85 *Pipe under the bubble*

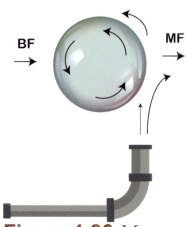

Figure 1.86 *Magnus force movement (MF)*

The Ghost Bubble:

Once you master the floating bubble you can create and observe one of the rarest bubbles, the elusive Ghost Bubble!

The reason that this faint outline of a bubble is so rarely seen is that bubbles will hit something and pop before they reach this fragile stage.

By gently blowing air under the bubble you can accomplish something unique.

Figure 1.87 illustrates the four stages of the bubble life and are explained below.

1. When a bubble comes off of a wand it is most often the colorful bubble we are all familiar with. When hanging from a wand the water will quickly move to the bottom of the bubble producing rings of color. But because the bubble is floating, and because you are blowing upwards and spinning it a bit, the thickness of the bubble stays fairly equal.

2. As the bubble floats the water in it will evaporate causing the bubble wall to get thinner. The light that is reflected by the thin film will change to a golden color.

3. As more water evaporates the bubble will no longer reflect light as a thin film but simply be clear, and reflect light like any glass or other smooth surface.

4. If it survives long enough the water will almost completely evaporate from the bubble leaving the polymers and soap in the form of a shell held together by the few remaining water molecules. This bubble might be barely visible.

5. This is the ghost bubble.

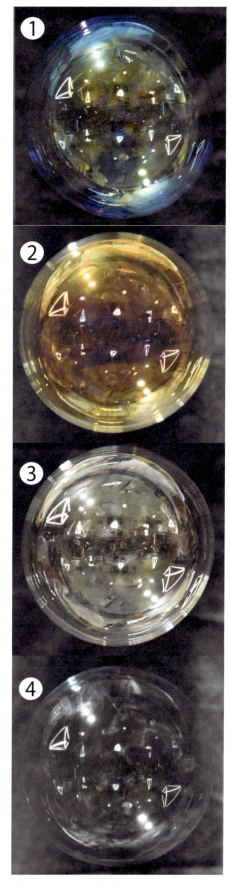

Figure 1.87 *Four stages of the life of a bubble*

Reflections in bubbles:

One of the fun thing about bubbles is seeing yourself reflected. You will notice two images in the bubble. One of the images will be enlarged and distorted. The other image will be upside down.

The clearest image is often the source of light. Many of these images show the bank of long tube lights used to illuminate the objects and you will notice some on the top and some on the bottom of the bubble.

In Figure 1.88 you can see the two images of the author. The light must be bright enough to illuminate the subject and the background must be dark enough not to overpower the reflected light in order to get a clear image.

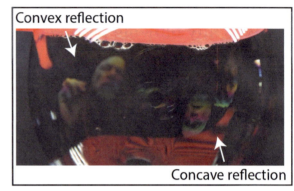

Figure 1.88 *Two reflections in each bubble*

To understand the images each part of the bubble is looked at separately.

- The front side of the bubble behaves like a convex mirror.
- A convex mirror (Figure 1.89) will cause reflected light to spread out from a single point, known as a **focal point**.
- The image produced by a convex mirror is smaller than the object, and right side up.

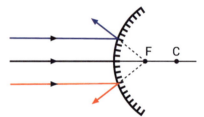

Figure 1.89 *Convex mirror ray diagram*

- The back side of the bubble behaves like a concave mirror.
- A concave mirror (Figure 1.90) will cause reflected light to come together towards a focal point and then move outward.
- The image produced by a concave mirror is larger than the object, and up side down.

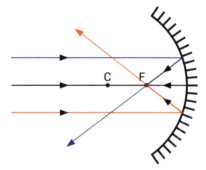

Figure 1.90 *Concave mirror ray diagram*

a) Look at your reflection in a spoon, both front and back of the spoon.

b) Move it further away and see what changes.

Because the bubble can easily change its shape the focal points and images will also change. This produces the images you see in a bubble.

Bubble colors:

The colors of bubbles were observed and explained by Issac Newton in 1704. This explanation is known as **Newton thin film interference**.

- Newton suggested that light traveled as a wave.
- Waves can interfere with each other to make some stronger and some weaker.
- The color of the light depends upon the length of these waves and each color has a different wavelength.
- The thin film causes some light to reflect off the front surface, and other light to reflect off the back surface.
- These two beams can interfere making some wavelengths stronger and, with light, that makes it brighter.
- The thickness of the thin film determines which wavelengths of light will interfere to make a specific color brighter (Figure 1.91).
- As the thickness of the film changes the colors that are seen also changes.

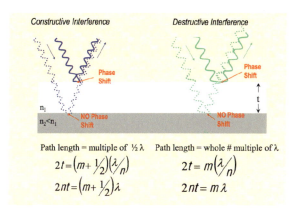

Figure 1.91 *Thin film interference producing colors*

Going much further

- In 1905 Albert Einstein showed that light did not travel in waves but in little packets he called 'quanta'.
- The explanation of how these quanta interact is talked about in a very strange part of science known as quantum physics.
- The explanation of colors in bubbles is so mathematically complex (Figure 1.92) that Newton interference is still taught today.
- In both explanations the colors of light you see is determined by the thickness of the thin film.

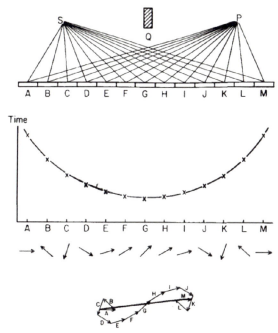

Figure 1.92 *Vector resolution of quantum probability amplitudes*

Photographing bubbles:

a) Blow a bubble on the extra wand.

b) Hold the bubble against a light colored background. The light reflected from the bubble is not as bright as the light coming through the bubble.

c) Hold the same bubble against a dark colored background. The light from the bubble stands out more (Figure 1.93).

Figure 1.93 *Light background (1) and dark background (2)*

- When photographing bubbles it is very important to keep the background in mind (Figure 1.94).
- The light source that illuminates the bubble is also important.
- Too much light and the bubble is overcome with brightness.
- As is seen with a light table, light from below is often useful.

Figure 1.94 *Cluttered background*

Another problem when trying to take photographs of bubbles is the focus.

Cell phone cameras have an auto focus that automatically focuses on the 'subject' in the center of the photo. This can be a problem because the bubble itself is usually clear and is difficult to focus.

Figure 1.95 *Well composed photo of young bubble artists*

The secret to taking a good photograph of a bubble is to be aware of the lighting, focus and background, and then to take a lot of photos to try and capture the perfect combination.

Make a light table:

The light table can add a lot to a simple bubble on a plate. By using an inexpensive 'infinity light', which is a self contained light decoration, under the clear bubble plate you can get some amazing light effects reflected off of your bubble (Figure 1.96). This can be done with any light source that is placed under the clear bubble plate.

Figure 1.96 *Plate on infinity light.*

- A simple home made light table (Figure 1.97) can be made with a round 'photo' light and an inexpensive plastic cake display stand. Many of these lights have fancy color effects.

- Some artists use very large light tables. This allows for larger bubbles to be formed and can be a base upon which more complex structures are formed.

Figure 1.97 *Making a simple light table*

Your bubble kit came with a flashlight. This light can be positioned on the table next to the plate so that the light shines upward into the bubble form.

Using colored lights on a light table can add some dramatic effects to your bubbles however the colors reflected from the bubble originate from the light sources, and a white light will provide the most colorful bubbles.

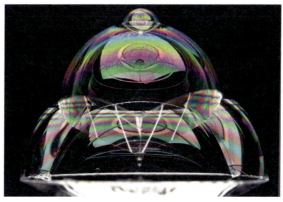

Figure 1.98 *Large clear plastic plate on a square light table.*

What is next?:

Now that you have a basic understanding of bubbles you are ready to begin a journey that may help you entertain your friends, or amaze the world.

Your first step should be to find the **Soap Bubble Wiki.**

And then practice a lot. Have fun.

Umar Shoaib and Pierre-Yves Fusier with light table

Tom Noddy's tornado bubble built by and photographed by Graham Maxwell

Chang Yu Te with pentagonal dodecahedron bubble (KOMMA)

Thomas GoodMan with vapor bubble with a 'hole' in it

Meadow Perry using a large frame device called a 'Bubble Wall'

What is next? More:

Steve Langley bubble chain (Jim McGuire Photography)

Florent Daron, Bourgogne, France

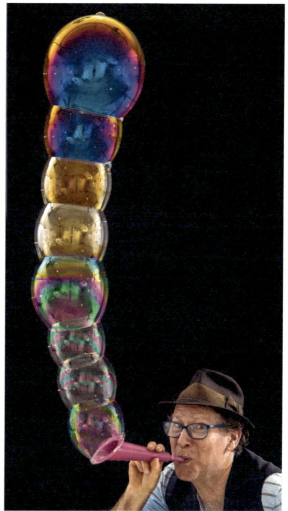

Louis Pearl using his famous Bubble Trumpet (Google it)

Pierre-yves Fusier, Paris France (Serge Guichard)

What is next? Bigger:

To entertain large crowds the tricks have to be big and dramatic. Giant bubbles and giant tricks require a lot of practice, but the results are worth it.

Clotilde Cloe long bubble

Dov Citron, London, England

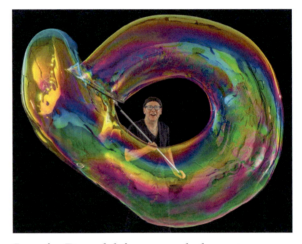

Louis Pearl big wand donut

Mike Gee, United Kingdom

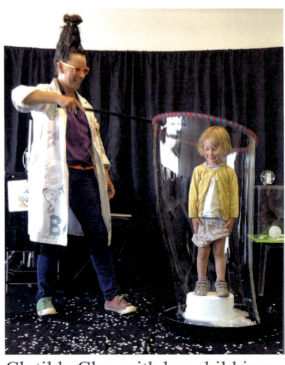

Clotilde Cloe with her child in a bubble.

What is next? More and bigger:

Many bubblers will use string based wands and their special mix to make large 'outdoor' bubbles. Using the wind to inflate the bubbles these majestic structures can fill the sky with iridescent beauty.

Bubble Net by Gordy Tobutt, Illinois, USA

Luca Cutrupi, Milan, Italy

Bubble Net by Gary Pearlman

Mary Jordan, Michigan, USA

Rick Findley, Guadalajara, Mexico, using a tri-string wand

Ian Russell, High Peak, UK

What is next? Imagination:

Chang Yu Te setting Guinness World Record (GWR)

Eran Backler

Matěj Kodeš setting GWR

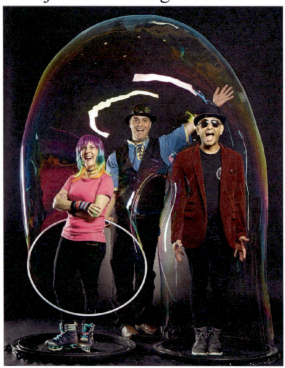

Caroline Cornelius-Jones, Eran Backler, Umar Shoaib

Moose in bubble (Clotilde Cloe)

What is next? Imagination:

Pierre-Yves Fusier, Paris France (Serge Guichard). If your hand is wet you can 'hold' the bubble.

Caroline Cornelius-Jones with her bubble umbrella

Damian Jay, Bubble wands

Thomas GoodMan with hand held cube and vapor tool

Carol Collins and friends

What is next? Imagination:

Paola Dyboski-Bryant and friends setting Guinness World Records (GWR)

Pierpaolo Laconi, Rome, Italy

Aelwfyn Shipton, UK

Rosemary Altman, Oswego, NY

Thomas C. Altman, Oswego, NY

ASSOCIATION OF INTERNATIONAL BUBBLE ARTISTES

The Association of International Bubble Artistes (AOIBA), was founded in 2019 -during a convention of Bubble Artistes from around the world. Their aim - to create an international community of practitioners who support, encourage and enhance the Art of Bubbling in all its forms and applications. To encourage safe and ethical practices through its code of conduct and its members shared experiences.

Everyone loves a bubble regardless of how they identify. The AOIBA and the worldwide Bubbler-Family are fully inclusive and embrace diversity.

Events like BubbleDaze and BubbleCon, as pictured here brought Bubble Artistes together from across the globe and were the catalyst for AOIBA.

Visit www.aoiba.org to find out more.

Apart from stage or outdoor performances at parties, events and theaters, bubbles can also be used as Therapy, bringing proven benefits, as well as huge smiles, to diverse groups of people.

Seeing and playing in new ways, a blind person discovers by touch.

Attributes:

The following members of AOIBA contributed to this manual and can be found on Facebook and other social media platforms.

Thomas C. Altman, Oswego, NY, USA. altmanscience.com. Author of 4 science text books, teacher 35 years, Science and bubble shows since 1985

Martin Aggerbeck has worked with soap bubbles and science for over 15 years. Copenhagen, Denmark. www.idefu.dk

Eran Backler; Auckland, New Zealand. A trained teacher and actor. Touring internationally with his Award-winning Bubble Show. www.highlandjoker.com

Iulia Benze: Europe (Romania-UK) and Australia https://adultbubbleshow.com Photography by Alf Knoll, skorpophoto

Melissa Bornmann (Bubbles McGee) is a Bubble Entertainer in the Greater Boston Area www.BubblesMcGee.com Melissa@BubblesMcGee.com

Greg Brinchault Bubbleshow, France.

Dov Citron: Captain Calamity, UK based entertainer children's books magic, balloons, science and bubbles to create a world of wonder in his touring shows.

Clotilde Cloe, French Canadian bubble artist, circus artist, Clown and magician, Montréal, Québec. +1-514-814-7086/ ClotildeCloe (Fb & Ig)

Carol Collins, Gainesville, Virginia, USA, Newventur Entertainment, LLC 50 Variety Acts/parties/events www.partyco-op.com

Caroline Cornelius-Jones aka CJ the Bubble Girl, an awarding winning bubble artiste in Singapore & Asia www.cjbubbles.com

Luca Cutrupi, Milan, Italy Luca is an Italian artist Bubbling since 2015 Around Italy and Europe Co-founder @ Incredibolle

Attributes:

Florent Daron, Bourgogne, France, Creator of smiles for children and adults.

Pierre-Yves Fusier (aka Slash Bubbles), Paris, France 3 GWR
www.slashbubblesparis.com
www.lacameleone.com
Bubble shows or Theatre play

Martin Cattani Dorelo Cia. Enlaire Catalunya -Spain
www.ciaenlaire.com

Mike Gee (BubbleMan), with Lucy Tunc (Bubble Faerie), UK, Performs for all types of events home or abroad.
Facebook.com/rainbowgecko

Helen Dutch: Helen (Daffy Dill) loves to bring joy to Events Performing in her Incredibubble Bubble Show With Mirth Magic and More

Aramis Gehberger performs worldwide since 2009. Indoor, Outdoor, Interactive shows and more. GWR 2019
www.bubbleshow.at

Paola Dyboski-Bryant is the founder of Dr Zigs, manufacturer and retailer of environmentally friendly Bubble toys worldwide.

Thomas GoodMan: Italy
bollestrabelle@gmail.com
@bollestrabelle on Instagram
@thomasgoodman.
raccontabolle on facebook

Rick Findley; " I always try to make each of my bubbling sessions interactive, especially with children. Their innocent wizardry can surprise"

Sam Heath: Samsam Bubbleman-bubbling since 1989. Runs Bubble Inc -toy brand & international bubble entertainment. 12 GWR

Shirley Freeman is a UK bubble performer doing outdoor shows with Memorabubble and also a bubble photographer.

Damian Jay. A UK based bubble Artiste performing in shows and at events.
www.thebubbleshow.co.uk
Damian@damianjay.com

Attributes:

Mary Jordan, Michigan, USA. Fairs and Festivals Fairy Bubble Entertainer, outdoor and stage. Bubbling since 2014. www.FairyMary.net

Matěj Kodeš: professional bubbler and multiple GWR record holder from the Czech Republic. Available worldwide. www.bubbleshow.cz

Stephanie Krawinkler, Vienna, Austria, Social & cultural anthropologist, bubble geek, performance & visual artist. www.missbubblebliss.at

Pierpaolo Laconi: Rome, Italy Author of "Bubbles Art" www.whitedreamperformer.com

Steve Langley: Steve makes a very clean living playing with bubbles. He has done many cool things and received much recognition. 9 GWR

Graham Maxwell: Maxwell the Bubbleologist loves Bubbles.

Faris Nasir, Malaysia based multidisciplinary artist using soap bubbles, fire and 3D fractals as medium. linktr.ee/farisnasir

Tom Noddy: thebubbleguy@aol.com, continues a lifelong interest in the art and beauty of bubbles with both live and virtual performances.

Louis Pearl, aka Amazing Bubble Man. Over 8000 shows performed worldwide since 1980. When not on tour he resides in Portland, OR, USA.

Gary Pearlman from Cleveland Ohio is a professional bubbleologist and winner of 11 GWR. Www.drurawesome.com

Meadow Perry is a magician and actress from the USA. She tours with her original Bubble Magic show and lectures as an instructor for Bubble U.

Corinne Bubbles Powder (IT) Berlin, Germany www.bubblespowder.com Bubbles Artist since 2012

Attributes:

Dustin Reudelhuber, Oklahoma, USA
A full time award winning family entertainer who runs Tulsabubbles.com

Ian Russell is a science communicator who loves infecting people with his contagious delight in all natural phenomena.

Aelfwyn Shipton: Bristol, UK www.mirabellearts.com Bubblina is a bubbleologist combining bubbles and music in perfect harmony.

Umar Shoaib (aka Ray Bubbles) is a multiple world record holding bubble artist performing around Europe, training the artists of tomorrow.

Gordy Tobutt, Illinois, USA. Outdoor bubble equipment and entertainment. GlowbyTheBubbler.com

Chang Yu Te: (aka AN DY), Taiwan, 5 GWR by the age of 22, Uses few props and depends on innovation to teach understanding and love.

Photography: Steve Langley photo by Jim McGuire Photography
Photography: Photos of Tom Noddy by Michelle Bates

Photography: Louis Pearl photos by Mirifoto

Photography: Chang Yu Te photos by KOMMA

Photography: Stephanie Krawinkler bubbles in bubble photo by Matthias Leitzke

Photography: Pierre-Yves Fusier, photographer Serge Guichard

Photography: Thin film on cover and background of her attribute page taken by Stephanie Krawinkler.

Photography: Photographs of children used with written permission of parents.

Made in United States
Troutdale, OR
08/24/2024

22281474R00040